DK READERS

Pre-level 1

Fishy Tales
Colorful Days
Garden Friends
Party Fun
In the Park
Farm Animals
Petting Zoo
Let's Make Music
Meet the Dinosaurs
Duck Pond Dip

My Dress-up Box
On the Move
Snakes Slither and Hiss
Family Vacation
Ponies and Horses
John Deere: Busy Tractors
Lego Duplo: On the Farm
Cuentos de Peces *en español*
Dias Ilenos de color *en español*

Level 1

A Day at Greenhill Farm
Truck Trouble
Tale of a Tadpole
Surprise Puppy!
Duckling Days
A Day at Seagull Beach
Whatever the Weather
Busy Buzzy Bee
Big Machines
Wild Baby Animals
A Bed for the Winter
Born to be a Butterfly
Dinosaur's Day
Feeding Time
Diving Dolphin
Rockets and Spaceships
My Cat's Secret
First Day at Gymnastics
A Trip to the Zoo
I Can Swim!
A Trip to the Library
A Trip to the Doctor
A Trip to the Dentist
I Want to be a Ballerina
Animal Hide and Seek
Submarines and Submersibles
Animals at Home
Let's Play Soccer

Homes Around the World
LEGO: Trouble at the Bridge
LEGO: Secret at Dolphin Bay
Star Wars: What is a Wookie?
Star Wars: Ready, Set, Podrace!
Star Wars: Luke Skywalker's Amazing
     Story
Star Wars Clone Wars: Watch Out for
     Jabba the Hutt!
Star Wars Clone Wars: Pirates... and
     Worse
Power Rangers: Jungle Fury: We are the
     Power Rangers
Lego Duplo: Around Town
Indiana Jones: Indy's Adventures
John Deere: Good Morning, Farm!
A Day in the Life of a Builder
A Day in the Life of a Dancer
A Day in the Life of a Firefighter
A Day in the Life of a Teacher
A Day in the Life of a Musician
A Day in the Life of a Doctor
A Day in the Life of a Police Officer
A Day in the Life of a TV Reporter
Gigantes de Hierro *en español*
Crías del mundo animal *en español*

A Note to Parents

DK READERS is a compelling program for beginning readers, designed in conjunction with leading literacy experts, including Dr. Linda Gambrell, Distinguished Professor of Education at Clemson University. Dr. Gambrell has served as President of the National Reading Conference, the College Reading Association, and the International Reading Association.

Beautiful illustrations and superb full-color photographs combine with engaging, easy-to-read stories to offer a fresh approach to each subject in the series. Each DK READER is guaranteed to capture a child's interest while developing his or her reading skills, general knowledge, and love of reading.

The five levels of DK READERS are aimed at different reading abilities, enabling you to choose the books that are exactly right for your child:

Pre-level 1: Learning to read
Level 1: Beginning to read
Level 2: Beginning to read alone
Level 3: Reading alone
Level 4: Proficient readers

The "normal" age at which a child begins to read can be anywhere from three to eight years old. Adult participation through the lower levels is very helpful for providing encouragement, discussing storylines, and sounding out unfamiliar words.

No matter which level you select, you can be sure that you are helping your child learn to read, then read to learn!

LONDON, NEW YORK, MUNICH,
MELBOURNE, AND DELHI

Series Editor Deborah Lock
Senior Art Editor Tory Gordon-Harris
Design Assistant Sadie Thomas
U.S. Editor Elizabeth Hester
Production Editor Sean Daly
Jacket Designer Natalie Godwin
Publishing Manager Bridget Giles

Reading Consultant
Linda Gambrell, Ph.D.

First American Edition, 2003
This edition, 2010
10 11 12 13 14 15 10 9 8 7 6 5 4 3 2 1
Published in the United States by DK Publishing
375 Hudson Street, New York, New York 10014

Published in Great Britain by Dorling Kindersley Limited

DK books are available at special discounts when purchased in bulk
for sales promotions, premiums, fund-raising, or educational use.
For details, contact: DK Publishing Special Markets
375 Hudson Street, New York, New York 10014
SpecialSales@dk.com

A catalog record for this book is available
from the Library of Congress

ISBN: 978-0-7566-6167-0 (pb)
ISBN: 978-0-7566-6168-7 (plc)

Color reproduction by Colourscan, Singapore
Printed and bound in China by L. Rex Printing Co. Ltd.

The publisher would like to thank the following for their kind
permission to reproduce their photographs:
a=above; c=center; b=below; l=left; r=right t=top;
Ardea London Ltd: 23tr; **Corbis:** Wolfgang Kaehler 13c. Rob C.
Nunnington/Gallo Images 28tl; **Philip Dowell:** 26-27; **Getty Images:**
Arthur S.Aubry 30-31; Geoff du Feu 10tl; David McGlynn 4cl; Laurence
Monneret 31c; Tom Schierlitz 27br; Bob Stefko 18l; Kevin Summers
20-21; **Natural History Museum:** 2cra, 7cbr, 24bl, 24br, 25bl, 25bc,
25bcr, 32tl, 32bl; **N.H.P.A:** Stephen Dalton 15tr; David Middleton
4-5; **Oxford Scientific Film:** 8tl, 8-9, 9tc, Claude Steelman/SAL 6-7;
Jerry Young: 11bc, 26bl;
Jacket images: *Front:* **Alamy Images:** D. Hurst
All other images © Dorling Kindersley
For further imformation see: www.dkimages.com

Discover more at
www.dk.com

DK READERS

LEARNING
pre-level
1
TO READ

Garden
Friends

DK Publishing

butterfly

garden

Meet the small animals in my garden.

snail

antenna

flower

butterflies

Hello, butterfly.
You are resting
on a flower.

wing

leaf

eye

mouth

 caterpillars

Hello, caterpillar.
You are eating
a big leaf.

spot

 ladybugs

Hello, ladybugs.
You have
many spots.

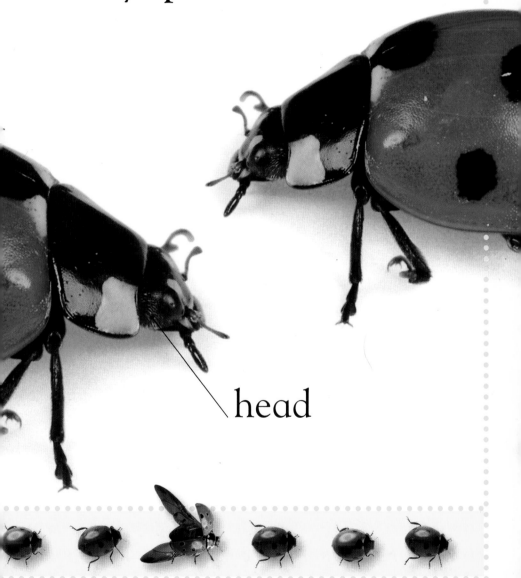

head

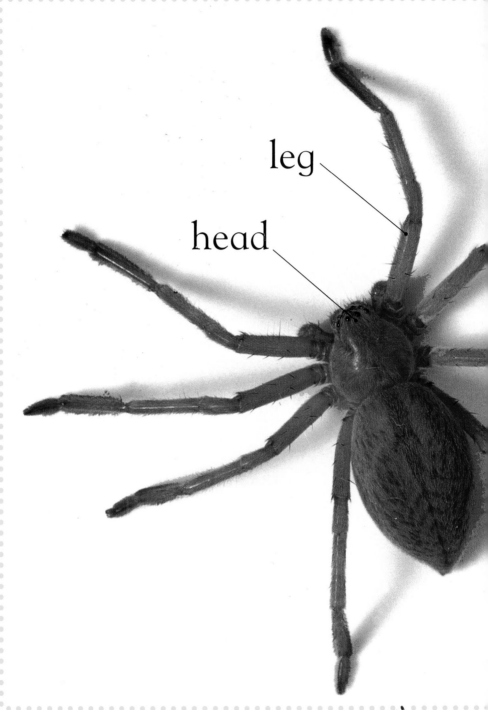

leg

head

 spiders

Hello, spider.
You have spun
a big web.

web

flower

furry body

 bumblebees

Hello, bumblebee.
You are drinking
from a flower.

Hello, centipede.
You have many legs.

centipedes

head

leg

Hello, dragonfly.
You are flying
around very fast.

 dragonflies

wing

leg

19

baby snail

shell

snails

Hello, snail.
You have a baby
on your back.

soft body

worms

Hello, worms.
You are very long.

Hello, stag beetle.
You have very
sharp jaws.

wing

head

jaw

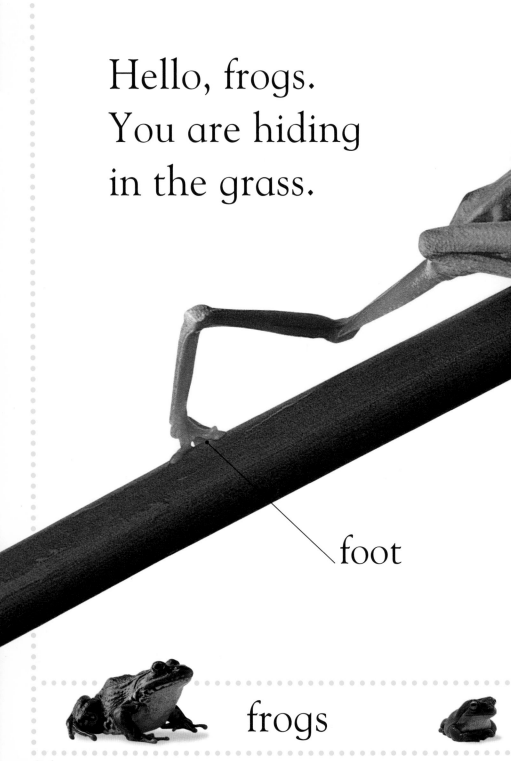

Hello, frogs.
You are hiding
in the grass.

foot

frogs

grasshoppers

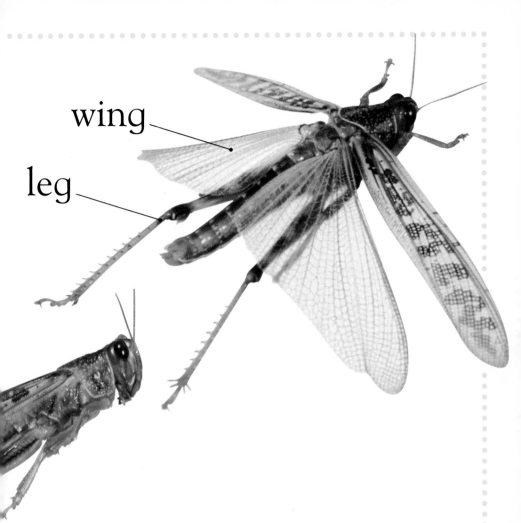

wing

leg

Hello, grasshoppers.
Wow!
What a big jump!

dragonfly

 What animals can

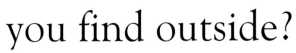 you find outside?

Glossary

Antennae are used by insects to feel their surroundings

Centipede an insect with many legs

Jaws are used by stag beetles to fight and nip

Shell the hard outside covering on some animals

Web some spiders make webs to catch prey, and as a place to rest

Index